Dear Parents and Educators,

Welcome to Penguin Young Readers! As parents and educators, you know that each child develops at his or her own pace—in terms of speech, critical thinking, and, of course, reading. Penguin Young Readers recognizes this fact. As a result, each Penguin Young Readers book is assigned a traditional easy-to-read level (1–4) as well as a Guided Reading Level (A–P). Both of these systems will help you choose the right book for your child. Please refer to the back of each book for specific leveling information. Penguin Young Readers features esteemed authors and illustrators, stories about favorite characters, fascinating nonfiction, and more!

| Red, White, and Blue
 The Story of the American Flag | LEVEL **3**
 GUIDED READING LEVEL **M** |

This book is perfect for a **Transitional Reader** who:
• can read multisyllable and compound words;
• can read words with prefixes and suffixes;
• is able to identify story elements (beginning, middle, end, plot, setting, characters, problem, solution); and
• can understand different points of view.

Here are some **activities** you can do during and after reading this book:
• Comprehension: Answer the following questions:
    • How many colonies were represented on the first American flag?
    • Who was Francis Scott Key?
    • What holiday is celebrated on June 14?
    • How many stars and stripes are on our flag today?
• Research: Use the Internet to do your own research on the history of another country's flag.

Remember, sharing the love of reading with a child is the best gift you can give!

—Bonnie Bader, EdM
    Penguin Young Readers program

*Penguin Young Readers are leveled by independent reviewers applying the standards developed by Irene Fountas and Gay Su Pinnell in *Matching Books to Readers: Using Leveled Books in Guided Reading*, Heinemann, 1999.

Penguin Young Readers
Published by the Penguin Group
Penguin Group (USA) Inc., 375 Hudson Street, New York, New York 10014, USA
Penguin Group (Canada), 90 Eglinton Avenue East, Suite 700, Toronto, Ontario M4P 2Y3, Canada
(a division of Pearson Penguin Canada Inc.)
Penguin Books Ltd., 80 Strand, London WC2R 0RL, England
Penguin Group Ireland, 25 St. Stephen's Green, Dublin 2, Ireland (a division of Penguin Books Ltd.)
Penguin Group (Australia), 250 Camberwell Road, Camberwell, Victoria 3124, Australia
(a division of Pearson Australia Group Pty. Ltd.)
Penguin Books India Pvt. Ltd., 11 Community Centre, Panchsheel Park, New Delhi—110 017, India
Penguin Group (NZ), 67 Apollo Drive, Rosedale, Auckland 0632, New Zealand
(a division of Pearson New Zealand Ltd.)
Penguin Books (South Africa) (Pty.) Ltd., 24 Sturdee Avenue,
Rosebank, Johannesburg 2196, South Africa

Penguin Books Ltd., Registered Offices: 80 Strand, London WC2R 0RL, England

Library of Congress Control Number: 97033413

ISBN 978-0-448-41270-2

Red, White, and Blue

The Story of the American Flag

by John Herman
illustrated by Robin Roraback

Penguin Young Readers
An Imprint of Penguin Group (USA) Inc.

We all know the American flag. Its
bright colors fly at baseball games.

It flies at Fourth of July parades.

We even see it on clothes!

Our flag has lots of nicknames—like Old Glory and the Red, White, and Blue. Sometimes it's called the Stars and Stripes. But where did our flag come from? Who decided what it would look like? The truth is that no one knows for sure.

Back in the 1700s, America didn't have a flag. It didn't need one. It wasn't even a country yet.

It was just 13 colonies. The colonies belonged to England. The English flag flew in towns from New Hampshire to Georgia.

But as time went on, the 13 colonies didn't want to belong to England anymore. Americans decided to fight for their freedom.

A war began. It was the American Revolution. Now a new flag was needed—an American flag.

Who made our first flag? Some people say it was a woman named Betsy Ross. Maybe you've heard of her. Betsy Ross owned a sewing shop in Philadelphia. She was famous for her sewing.

The story is that one day a general came to see her. The general was George Washington. He was the head of the American army.

General Washington wanted a new
flag. It would make his soldiers feel like
a real army fighting for a real country.

He wanted Betsy Ross to make
this flag. He drew a picture of what
he wanted.

Betsy Ross made some changes.
Then she showed the picture to
General Washington. He liked it!

Betsy Ross sewed the flag. And that was the very first Stars and Stripes.

That is the story—and it's a good
one. But is it true? Betsy Ross's
grandson said it was. He said that
Betsy told him the story when he
was a little boy and she was an old
woman of 84. But there is no proof
for this story. So what do we know
for sure?

We know that during the Revolution, the colonists used lots of different flags.

But once the colonies became the United States of America, the country needed *one* flag—the same flag for everybody.

So on June 14, 1777, a decision was made. The flag was going to have 13 red and white stripes. The flag was also going to have 13 white stars on a blue background, one for each of the 13 colonies.

Now the United States had a flag. Congress had picked the colors and the stars and stripes. But Congress did not say where the stars and stripes had to go. So the flag still did not always look the same!

People could put them any way they liked. Sometimes the stripes were up and down, like this.

Sometimes the stars were in a circle, like this.

But nobody minded. Up and down
or side to side, the stars and stripes
still stood for the United States.

Over the years, the flag became more and more important to people. In 1812, the United States was at war with England again. British soldiers came to America. They sailed up our rivers.

They marched down our
streets. They even burned down
the White House—the home of
the president.

On the night of September 13, 1814, British soldiers bombed a fort in Maryland. All that night a man watched the fighting. His name was Francis Scott Key. He was afraid. What if the American soldiers in the fort gave up?

But in the early morning light,
he saw the Stars and Stripes. It was
still flying above the fort! He knew
American soldiers had won the battle.

Key felt very proud. He wrote a poem about the flag on the fort. The poem was "The Star-Spangled Banner." Later the poem was put to music. This song about our flag became a song for our whole country.

The flag that Francis Scott Key saw had 15 stripes and 15 stars.

Why? Because by then there were two more states—Vermont and Kentucky.

Our country was getting bigger. People were heading out west. In time, more places were going to want to be states. Soon there would be too many stripes to fit on the flag! Congress had to do something.

So in 1818 this is what was decided: The flag would go back to 13 red and white stripes. And in the blue box would be one white star for each state. Every time there was a new state, a new star would be added.

The United States in 1850

This map shows all the states as of 1850.

CALIFORNIA

At last the Stars and Stripes looked the same everywhere it flew. And Americans were proud of their flag. They took the flag with them as they moved west. The flag crossed the Mississippi River and the great, grassy plains and the Rocky Mountains. It made it all the way to California.

More and more states were added to the country. And more and more stars were added to the flag. By 1837, there were 26 stars on the flag. By 1850, there were 31.

One country. One flag. But then in 1861, something happened. Our country split in two. Eleven states in the South broke away from the United States of America. They started their own country. It was called the Confederate (say: Con-FED-ur-it) States of America. Abraham Lincoln was president of the United States. He said *all* the states had to stay together.

War broke out—the Civil War. It was a very sad time in the history of our country.

The 11 southern states stopped
flying the Stars and Stripes. They
had their own flag.

In the North, some people wanted 11 stars taken off the Stars and Stripes. But Abraham Lincoln would not do that. He said the states would get back together. He was right. The Civil War ended in 1865. The North won. And the United States was one country under one flag again.

On June 14, 1877, the flag had a birthday—a big one. It was 100 years old.

All across the country, people had picnics and parties and parades. June 14 become a holiday—Flag Day.

Today our flag has 50 stars for the 50 United States of America. Some flags are huge.

One weighs 500 pounds! It is flown every Fourth of July from the George Washington Bridge.

The American flag flies in towns and cities from coast to coast. And that's not all. In 1969, two American astronauts were the first people ever to land on the moon. The astronauts took lots of moon rocks back to Earth. They also left something on the moon . . . the Stars and Stripes. And do you know what?

Our flag is still flying there!